The Lake Michigan Mermaid

Made in Michigan Writers Series

General Editors

Michael Delp, Interlochen Center for the Arts
M. L. Liebler, Wayne State University

Advisory Editors

Melba Joyce Boyd
Wayne State University

Stuart Dybek
Western Michigan University

Kathleen Glynn

Jerry Herron
Wayne State University

Laura Kasischke
University of Michigan

Thomas Lynch

Frank Rashid
Marygrove College

Doug Stanton

Keith Taylor
University of Michigan

A complete listing of the books in this series can be found online at wsupress.wayne.edu

The Lake Michigan Mermaid

A Tale in Poems

Linda Nemec Foster and
Anne-Marie Oomen

Illustrated by
Meridith Ridl

Wayne State University Press
Detroit

ISBN 978-0-8143-4220-6 (hardcover)
ISBN 978-0-8143-4221-3 (e-book)

Library of Congress Control Number: 2017942152

Publication of this book was made possible by a generous gift from The Meijer Foundation.

 Additional support provided by Michigan Council for Arts and Cultural Affairs.

Published with the assistance of a fund established by Thelma Gray James of Wayne State University for the publication of folklore and English studies.

Wayne State University Press
Leonard N. Simons Building
4809 Woodward Avenue
Detroit, Michigan 48201-1309

Visit us online at wsupress.wayne.edu

To Lyla Marie Foster,

my granddaughter who loves touching the lake's waves
and hearing the songs they sing (LNF)

To Marijo Bakker and Pat Harpe,

for our shared sister love of big water, big waves (AMO)

Lyk

My name is Lykretia, meaning joy, but
I don't feel joy. They call me Lyk for short.

The name, Lyk, it freaks me out. *Like, Lyk, like* . . .
Friends say my name so much it turns into

stammer, something their tongues are searching for,
to make one thing *like* . . . some other random

thing. But they never really do compare.
It's just a word to fill the air, *like Lyk* . . .

nothing. Each day I wonder if there might
be a being out there, beyond that line

my mom calls the *thin blue lip of blue lake,*
a being who would say *Lyk* like the name

was meant to join one joyful thing to some
other joyful thing. Is there any one?

Hearing My Name

Perhaps you
heard my name in
your dream last night when the
lonely sound of
ice captured the waves
and silenced their song, which
danced in your heart—this song, this
echo of a stranger
like
like your own voice—
as if the dream
carried you to the lake and you heard me
in the captive water—*Phyliadellacia*—my name
and my song—daughter of the lake.

Four Rooms

Even in winter—mostly in winter—
this Lake Michigan stretch has been mine, though
my gram calls us *loaners*, not owners. She claims
earth and lake loaned this stretch to her—though title
says it's been ours six grammas back, all the way
to the black-haired Potawatomi.

Then Gram *loaned* dunes and cottage to her girl,
my mom, who was supposed to *loan* to me
when I grew up, to live here too, and take
care of her like she does Gram. But Mom's job
is running down. Gramma, too, is running
down, her mind like shifting grains of dune.

Dad's been gone so long only I mind.
There's nothing else left to go but this spit
of sand and ice, where I can look so far out,
be so gone from them.
              Mom showed me once
a picture of a real heart, like a *home*
with four rooms, she said, *like us*.

Some rooms have gone cold.

I walk our beach in wind, watch for new floes,
plate ice, and the white slush that shapes the caves.
Out there, rising from churning waves and winds,
something *is* that I do not know. I feel
it in the cool blue of new ice, in my
gramma's faraway eyes. I hear it in

my mother's breaking voice. I throw open
my arms, asking, asking . . . ? Cold wind sweeps in
where something connected should have been.

The Mermaid in the Lake

Away from the depth of oceans
               away from the edge of stark rocks

away from the dancing rivers
               away from the stillness of ponds

away from the green reeds of marshes
               away from the empty laughter of fountains

away from all the waters I have known

               I come to this lake, this blue pearl

I come to touch the bottom of its memory
               I come to trace its line of horizon

I come to sing of its clouds and their shadows
               I come to claim its shells and sand and gulls

I come to find loneliness and its daughter
               I come to find her

Inside the Ice Caves

Water-carved. Lake-shaped. Words my gram would use
to say how these caves of ice were made, as
though these strange words came from water language
only she knows, maybe from her long past,
which she holds secret, but I can tell she moans

inside, feels monster waves hollow pearled rooms
on shores that are not shores in winter but
currents of lake caught and stilled by some merking
so cunning and cold I too am now caught
in his freezing world—just how my life feels,

like everything gone hard, like it does
when the lake freezes. But in the ice caves
where I am never supposed to go, not
ever, where it is blue, calm, and dangerous,
I perch in the shelter of a cave's mouth,

rest on this ice lip, stare over dark-iced
water not yet scarred by floes, stare through shell
light, frayed, fractured, toward a living being.
Someone's out there. I hold this ice place close,
learning how cold grows, that warmth will steal
my empty hope and melt it into deeps.

Inside the Lake's Heart

I cannot enter the world
that borders mine—the world
of swash and sea grass,
driftwood and beach fire.

Your world—young girl
with swift legs—is a mystery
to me. You explore ice caves,
blue and calm and dangerous.
I can barely see their hollow forms, these caves
that could be the chambers of your heart.

Let me describe the only heart I know,
the lake's heart of ebb and flow, constant
change. I cannot imagine anything calm—

only the heart that can never be seen.

After Supper

Mom says end of summer
we'll sell the cottage, move
to town, live in a rented house
near the big hospital.

Gramma and I cry for a long time,
me pacing the braided rug, Gram rocking
in the willow rocker, and Mom
putzing at the leaky sink,

cleaning up canned walleye
and frozen peas. I tell her
I'll get a job and give her all the money,
that I'll even babysit, which I hate.

She doesn't listen until I tell her
I'll steal something I can sell
for real money—I'll save us that way.
After she slaps me hard, she cries too.

Hearing You Cry

I heard everything—
the shouting rose above the waves—
                    grandmother's tears
mother's silence
                    daughter's pleading
mother's silence

until the sound
of the mother's hand
on her daughter's face
shook my body as if the lake
had been struck by lightning,
                    as if her face was my face.

Dear girl, who lives beyond my world,
I see you.   I hear you.   I know you.

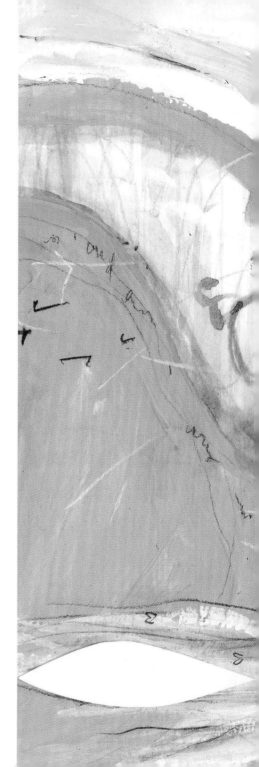

Will She Show Herself?

I sneak outside at night. How do I let her, the one
    out there, know that I am here,
        facing her riptides and breakers,
    her storm—
I am out here in rain and spitting snow.
    Showing myself.
        I promise I won't hurt you.
    Then I trip
on matted dune grass, roots storm-yanked from sand,
    like dream-tangled hair, uncombed. I pull free
        my own blue hair ribbons,
    tie them to the roots and grass.
Toss them to the undertow.
    A knot, a message to her,
        a ribbon word caught in the current.
    Recognition.

The Girl from Another World

I wave to the girl on the shore
and call her name in the wind.

Can she see me?
Can she hear me?
Can she know that I grieve
for her in that earth-bound home?
Its small doors and smaller windows,
its pale walls covered with forgotten landscapes.

She lives in a house filled with the voices
of women, but she cannot hear me,
the lake woman, the mermaid.

I want to give her some proof that I exist, a piece
of my world: the scattering of pearled colors,
lake shells on the beach for her to discover.

Sudden

Far out, a flash . . . a fish? But not. A sleek
and leaping thing, an arc alive, painted
morning fog, golden gray,

then low, a humming, almost
song. Gram hums along . . .
You—out there—

I can't see you, can't see past
that flash, light on light, strange dance.
But I hear you—

not the distant freighter
that fills the morning's foggy air—
not the muffled gulls—

your sound runs under that thrum,
almost a syllable, a splash, the lake,
made of glass, trying to speak . . .

spring. That sudden syllable.
Gram raises her head,
"Quick, too quick," she says.

What I Almost Say

No—it should be
what I almost sing
since plain speech eludes me—
my mouth fills with water
not words—songs of the waves
are the closest thing
to language I possess

in winter my voice is silent
a frozen wave

in spring I am the water
you dream about—
water   water
whispering
in each heartbeat of the moon.

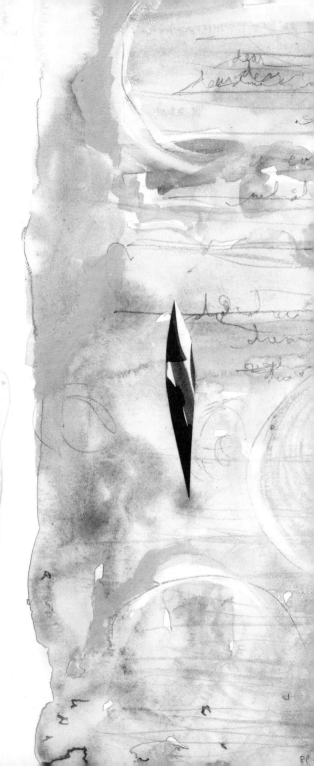

For Sale Sign

My mother plants the sign at the end of the driveway,
which is the end of the road. I shrug, *OK,*
who the heck comes way out here?

But then she pounds another on the shore
where boat people are bound to see it more.

Twice, I take it down before she catches me.
She looks mad, shoves it upright in the sand,
walks back to the cottage without a word.

Gram's restless with the change of light and air; she
walks back in time, all night long, up and down

the hall, ends up on the porch, staring out,
as though she sees someone she's known.
She tries to raise her arms and flag the air,

signaling. I think it's just that ugly sign
hurting her old heart. But maybe

it's the dream we share: that we could swim
without breathing air,
that we could have the kind of lungs

and heart a mermaid has
and breathe only water.

Sign?

What is this sign that faces the water?

Two words that cause an old woman
to forget who she is and sleepwalk
like a child. Two words that force
her daughter to ignore the sound
of waves and retreat to a place
of stone. Two words that make
her daughter's daughter dream
of the impossible: to live in my world.

World of pondweed, naiad, shell.
World of lake trout, pike, bluegill.

She dreams of entering this place,
wants to astonish the water

and the abandoned shore.

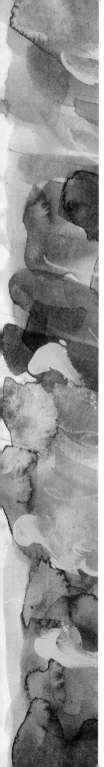
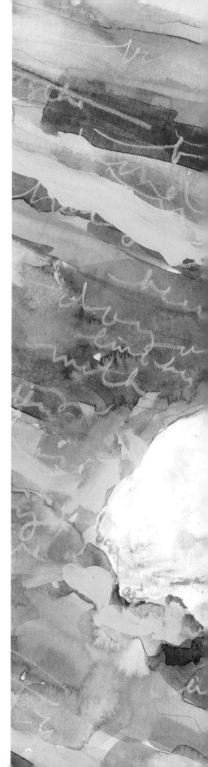

The Board

Who would think a piece of Styrofoam
could sweep me away, make me anything but me.
Storm washed it up, big enough to ride on.
I feel the waves under me and slip into blue swells.
I stand up, balance, almost a bird, and fly.

I know the deeps are deep.
But how far out are you, the one I know is there?
How far would I have to fly to hear your song?
How long before I would find you?
I think of this each time I fall and turn into a fish.

Mom says this game's dangerous, and she's right.
But every day I learn another steadiness,
how the wind will carry the board through chop.
Now I use the broken oar from the old boat
Daddy sold before he left. With it, I steer and soar.

I feel the currents cradle me.
I feel the wind turn me to a sail.
I like these feelings better than I like myself.
I skim the waves out where blue meets blue,
but I always come back to me, alone.

Out on the deeps where the water turns
night cruel, where there is no bottom,
only that ragged surface,
the froth makes white lines
like letters for her . . .

First Words of Another Language

. . . letters that I want to write.
Those words (you say) I hold
in my cool palms. I wish
I could speak your language
in the same way I whisper to the moon:

songs of deep water and calm. But I cannot.

The foam from my flowing hair
tries to write your name—*Girl*
Who Walks on the Shore. But the words
get lost in the waves. Finally, I weave
pale shells in the braid of blue ribbons you tossed
into the lake. My quiet language leaves
the water to reach your hands,
your ears. *Listen.*   *Listen.*   *I'm here.*

Skippers

This week, twice, the cops brought Gram back here,
and twice she turned on the kettle for tea
and forgot. Mom came home from what small
work she's got, and me from school, to sirens
and melted metal all over the stove. Scared mad.
Cops said, "Lucky." Now Mom says she can't do it.
Gramma has to go to a "home." I threw all
the dishes down the stairs and called her a witch.
Gram hummed at the window and waved.

I skitter smooth stones out over the waves,
try to make my heart slow down,
count how the stones touch and skip, touch and skip . . .
One, two, three, four . . . rooms that sink. One for each.
Gram, Mom, Dad, land. I want them back.
If I just knew how to make it true.
And that's when I see the old dune roots, the mat
I tied my ribbons to . . . long weeks ago.
To each tattered ribbon is knotted a small
sweetwater shell, all creamy and curved like
a palm, a tiny bowl, empty but for hope.

Full Breath of Joy and Absence

Old woman, I hear you are gone.
Your life separated from the young girl
like the lake's edge from the land's shore.

I know you know me—have sensed my presence
over the years. Ever since that day long ago
when you caught a glimpse, a reflection,
a shimmer of my translucent skin, my hair

tangled in the waves' foam. Only once you saw me,
but that was enough to haunt your dreams,
to entice your granddaughter to seek me.

Now, with you gone, locked away in a small room,
will the young girl find her true self?
Make sense of her world—the land and the water—
with all its full breath of joy and absence?

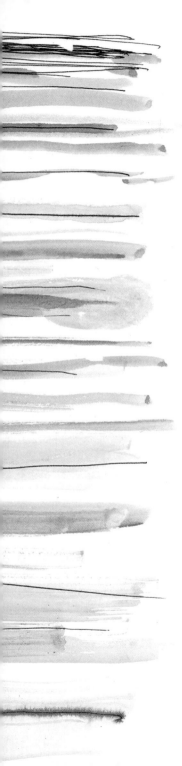

The Way

The board is too light for these winds, wobbly
          in the lee of this riptide, but I drag
it out as far as the sandbar anyway.
          My jeans soak through, my hands numb up in chill.

I don't care; I climb on, balance on my knees,
          as though to say my prayers. Wind catches,
an easterly, pushes me out under
          the moon. I let it go without a paddle,

out to the cold bone of freshwater sea,
          where just maybe she will be. She's got to be
all Gram dreamed before she left, every
          murmur about that moon she saw all those

years ago that changed her spirit. Now moon
          shows me that straight line they call horizon.
That word sounds like *rise and shine*, but it divides
          me from who I was and who I am to be.

Or never will be.
          I am near her.
It is so cold here. The waves,
          rising, comfort me.

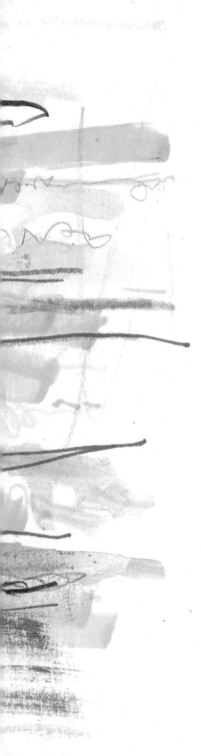

Your Face Reflected in Mine

Look down into the midnight water
    and see me. Your face above, mine below.
        Our contours mirror each other. The girl
            who loves the water merged with the girl

who lives within. Can you imagine me
    without silver scales or long hair encrusted
        with shells? Can I imagine you

without the miracle of legs or two feet
    touching the cool beach? Yes and No.
        No and Yes. We border two worlds
            like twin daughters of different mothers.

Yours, a woman of dried wildflowers.
    Mine, a shadow of aquamarine.
        Their separate dreams try to keep us strangers.

The Fall

The wind's a bully, won't let me turn, keeps pushing out.
I'm cold to my heart, too far from shore.
The gusts herd me hard, west, across the lake.
I can't see land, ours or any.

I've heard of this, so cold your skin turns warm,
then hot. I call for help, but no one hears
in storm. The only choice is to let go,
let go. That's when I hear her hum, and look down.

She is there, all silver-blue and green-haired song,
And I fall I fall I fall I fall I fall
all the way in, all the way down, all ways
into her arms, into the arms of the lake.

Lullaby

Before I see you falling, falling
into my world, I feel your essence.
I hear your muted gasps. I answer
with a song, a hint of a lullaby:

> Hush, hush, hush;
> be calm—don't struggle.
> Let go of all fear, all longing.

I am here, holding you, lifting you up
from the depths of my lake song
with its low melody, to the air
that surrounds your world of rock and driftwood.

> From your mother's dark sea, you first emerged.
> Now, feel the air caress your face again,
> as if for the first time.

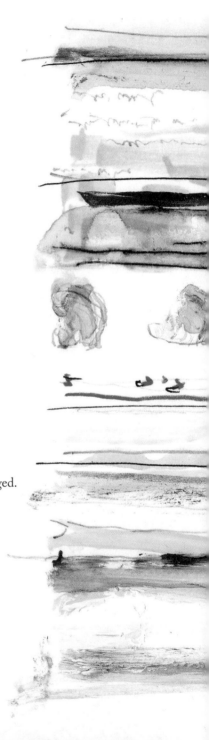

Her Hair

When I open my eyes—
        it is my mom
who's looking down at me.
        I choke and spit,
and she rolls me over,
        pushes on my back
until I throw up.
        I find my fists, I
shriek and strike at her.

I want her back, the other
        one who held
me softly and coldly.
        I burn with change.
Then Mom sings a song,
        not the one I heard
but maybe close enough,
        and my breathing calms.
How do mothers
        know these things?

When did her hair turn so gray?
        Like matted grass at summer's end,
and her eyes so sad?
        Then she says, "It's gone,
the land, the house,
        sold and done."
She sees then, I am also gone from her,
        lets go of my hand,
says so gently
        it cuts my heart,
"Not you too.
        I can't lose you too."

Why is every breath
        like a first, like a fist,
searing and deep,
        and water forced?
Oh water wish—hush, hush.

Lament

I gave you back to your life
to free you from mine. That freedom
has taken you far away from the rush
of the lake's breeze and the crash of its waves.

Far away from me. Girl, who was never my daughter,
how can I tell you there is a part of me
in your heart? The heart that longs to know
how far it is to the bottom, how the sun

can break itself into gemstones of amethyst,
citron, garnet, and amber. A sunset breaking
in your hand. My heart broken

in your leaving. Farewell to the girl
who casts her words into my waters. Farewell
to her silent mother, her grandmother lost in my past.

The Room Weeps

The room weeps of urine and wet linen,
other fates than mine. I sit next to Gram's chair,
where she mostly sleeps and pines.

I tell her I almost drowned in the deeps.
I was brought back by her. "Which one?" she asks.
"Mermaid? Or your mother?"

I ask myself at last. *Did both?*
Yes, I think both. I give her the mermaid's shells,
still strung on root and ribbons like moths.

I spread them on her blue blanket, thrown
over her knees. She fingers each one,
picks up, puts down, makes a pattern

on the weave. She lifts one, says,
"This one is broken for you . . ." then halts,
but I can finish her thoughts,

. . . by my father's hollow bottle. Mom asked
him to leave, so I would never know.
Brave mother indeed.

She picks another. "Your mother's fear . . ."
. . . for your care and mine, knotted
like a ship's tangled line.

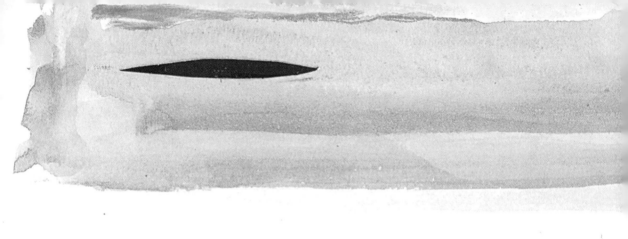

Another, and I see the land
and cottage, and the golden lie that
it was ours at all, to keep or sell.

She lifts a half of something whole.
"This is loss . . ." Her whisper cracks.
"But this remains . . ." She gropes, holds out

her empty hand, cupped, and places mine
against it, two, a whole but hollow thing.
The mermaid's spirit inside our palms—

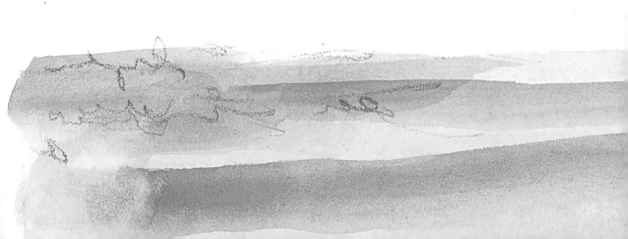

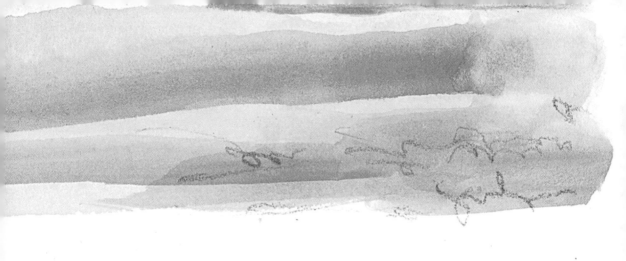

it asks we pay attention to her lake,
to her water, never to forsake
its beauty, to keep it well for her.

She carries on, "I too was once . . ." It's gone,
. . . *her daughter of water.*
I'm the new daughter, stronger

for having drowned, for having been
pulled in, pulled out. The waves
hit the shores inside me now.

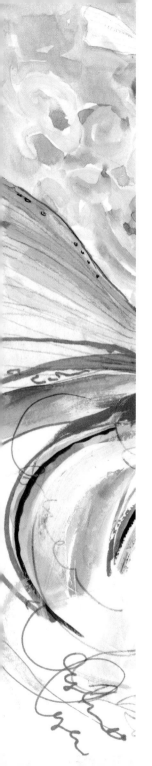

The Mermaid Enters the Girl's Dream

I enter your dream with my silver skin,
my blue/green hair married to the lake. I sing
a ballad—low chant of the moon—about a woman
who wrapped herself in silence, who refused
to listen to my song. The woman is your mother.
Her heart broken so many times, she transformed it
into an ice cave. Frozen like the lake's embrace
in winter. In the dream, you walk inside the cave
and discover a crystal labyrinth as elaborate
as a chambered nautilus. Remember this dream
when you awaken to the world. Your mother
lost in that spiral but her heart desperate
to be the shell singing in your ear. She may be mute,
but you'll know the song. *I have taught you the melody.*

Contrapuntal: *Two Voices of the Lake*

Say my name

       Call out the lake that lives in me,

and I will tell you

       because I love the waves,

the secrets of freshwater,

       the water running in wild currents,

secrets of falling and rising,

       the thirst for beauty in my ordinary life,

the sun and the moon,

the ebb and the flow—

traveling their journeys

that need no map

through the deep blue water

because they know they are home

Afterword

Throughout world mythologies, and particularly among the cultures of native peoples, mermaid tales abound. In modern times, the mermaid of the great oceans dominates our cultural consciousness, but stories of freshwater mermaids and mermen do exist. So we asked ourselves, is there a Lake Michigan mermaid, and if so, what is she like?

And who would ask such a question? The girl, Lyk, would. Anne-Marie heard her voice.

And who would answer such a question? The Lake Michigan mermaid would. Linda heard that voice.

And Meridith Ridl, bless her, knew just what they looked like.

In 2006, Linda and Anne-Marie both submitted pieces to a wonderful anthology, *Fresh Water: Women Writing on the Great Lakes*, and in 2008 they participated in a group reading from the book at the Saugatuck Center for the Arts. They sat next to each other at the event, warmly reacquainting after several years of watching and admiring each other's careers and writing. In the course of the readings, someone said that it was too bad there were no Lake Michigan mermaids. Linda and Anne-Marie looked at each other in surprise and wonder. Then with that inquisitive way that Linda has, she asked, "Are there really no Lake Michigan mermaids?" And Anne-Marie, in her practical way, said, "Well, there should be." They smiled, and nothing else might have happened except Anne-Marie had a long drive home. And while she was driving, her thoughts drifted to the mermaid, to the idea of the mermaid, and the more she thought about it, the more she believed the mermaid was a water story that Linda would understand.

So right there, on US-31 north, late at night, she called Linda and told her she had an exciting idea: they should write mermaid poems. Together. Or rather, they should write two sets of poems between a young girl and a mermaid. Linda felt a desire to write the mermaid's poems, and Anne-Marie felt that her voice was suited for the young girl's poems. They agreed they would write the poems one at a time, back and forth to each other, trading poems once a month. Sometimes they would write three or four at a time. Sometimes life got in the way, and they didn't write the mermaid poems for quite a few months. But they never forgot about the mermaid. By 2014, they had about eighteen poems, and they both felt the sequence taking shape, its meaning becoming clearer with every new piece.

In August of that year, they planned to spend a weekend writing additional mermaid poems to complete the project. Linda found a hotel in Manistee, a lakeshore town, and they rented a room right on Lake Michigan with a view of the beach and the pier, where they both could imagine the young girl on the shore and the mermaid in the distance. And with every word, these two voices became more real. Linda sat on the bed to write, and Anne-Marie sat on the picnic table outside the room. Anne-Marie liked to write early in the day, exploring the girl's world. Linda worked quietly at night, discovering the mermaid's voice. Through the weekend, they wrote and reviewed the manuscript poem by poem, and finished the draft (about sixteen more poems) by the end of that weekend. They felt the mermaid's story rising through it all, and the weather held so they could see the lake, their greatest influence and inspiration, every day.

After the weekend, they drove back to their homes but continued to revise the poems via e-mail. Late that fall, Anne-Marie contacted her wonderful editor, Annie Martin, at Wayne State University Press in Detroit, and they sent her the mermaid manuscript. In the summer of 2015, Annie wrote to say that the Press liked the poems but asked Anne-Marie and Linda to work on polishing the collection. The two poets met again to work on the revision of the manuscript and the sequence was then accepted for publication.

Then another challenge rose. Both Linda and Anne-Marie envisioned the book with illustrations, but not just any—rather with some mysterious and beautiful images of their beloved lake and waters. And how did one depict the ephemeral spirit of the lake, the mermaid? They discovered Meridith Ridl, whose multimedia paintings reflected the loneliness and longing of both the mermaid and the girl. When she came on board as illustrator, Linda and Anne-Marie were thrilled that the mermaid who had been in their imaginations would finally come to light.

The authors would like to thank Carrie Teefey, Rachel Ross, Rebecca Emanuelsen, and the support from Wayne State University Press. They also thank their husbands and best friends, Tony Foster and David Early.

Artist's Statement

Earthiness and wateriness, discovery and loss, clarity and blurriness . . . the in-between: these are all elements that became part of making images for Anne-Marie and Linda's narrative and lyrical poems. I hoped that the rhythms of their words might be suggested by layers of color and texture and by the visual rhythms found in water, sky, or weathered wood. Repeated motifs invite additional associations . . . what are these arches (moons, scales, waves, parentheses), words (songs, letters, poems, prayers), horizontal layers (earth, water, strata, sky)? I was interested in a tone of longing and of care: images that include things faded, scattered, wrinkled, and worn might suggest impermanence and isolation or intimacy and connection. There is loss in this story but also hope. The girl is bundled up . . . against the cold and/or the world, but she listens, watches, and reaches out. The mermaid is a shape-shifter of sorts . . . her skin changes like time changes ours, like light changes the lake, like experiences change our worlds.

Meridith Ridl

About the Authors

Linda Nemec Foster is the founder of the Contemporary Writers Series at Aquinas College. She is also the author of nine collections of poetry including *Amber Necklace from Gdansk, Talking Diamonds, Listen to the Landscape,* and *Living in the Fire Nest*. Foster was selected to be the first poet laureate of Grand Rapids, Michigan, from 2003 to 2005.

Anne-Marie Oomen is the author of *Love, Sex and 4-H* (Next Generation Indie Award for Memoir), *House of Fields* and *Pulling Down the Barn* (both Michigan Notable Books), and *Uncoded Woman* (poetry), among others. She teaches at Solstice MFA at Pine Manor College, Interlochen's College of Creative Arts, and at conferences throughout the country.

About the Illustrator

Meridith Ridl is an artist and an art teacher with a BA from the College of Wooster and MFA from the University of Michigan. She is represented by Lafontsee Galleries in Grand Rapids, Michigan. Meridith lives with her wonderful husband, Brent, in Saugatuck, Michigan, and loves wandering the lakeshore and dunes much like Lyk.